DISCARD

ADVENTURE SPORTS

TRAIL BIKES and MOTOCROSS

David Jefferis

DISCARD

J
796.75
J
J

Warwick Press

Illustrated by:
Rhoda and Robert Burns
James Robins
Michael Roffe

Edited by:
Jackie Gaff

Text consultant:
Patrick Devereux

Photographs supplied by:
Action Plus Photography
Patrick Devereux
David Jefferis

Published in 1990 by Warwick Press,
387 Park Avenue South, New York, New York 10016.
First published in 1989 by Kingfisher Books.

Copyright © Grisewood & Dempsey Ltd. 1989.

All rights reserved
5 4 3 2 1

Library of Congress Catalog Card No. 89-17833
ISBN 0-531-19076-5

Printed in Spain

Contents

Trail blazing

■ From muddy country trail to rocky mountain track, off-road riding combines adventure and skill. Rough terrain demands tough machines, and trail bikes are designed to withstand more than the average hammering. When fitted with speedometer, horn, indicators, and lights, they are legal to ride on public highways — if you are old enough and have paid the road tax. Lightweight stripped-down bikes are specially built for motocross racing on dirt-track circuits.

▶ Motocross is a spectacular sport and great for onlookers, as they can get really close to the action — it's usually possible to stand within a few yards of the track.

▲ Trail biking can take you down country lanes, over rutted tracks and across bare rock. Concern for others is a part of country riding — enjoy the ride, but don't disturb other people or animals with noise or high speed.

▶ Among the many forms of off-road racing are trials events — competitions that test precision riding skills.

Looking at motorcycles

■ Motorcyles vary greatly in size, weight, and power. Generally, the bigger the engine, the more powerful the bike. Super-fast top speed is not a major goal for off-road bike designers though. Instead, engines are built for strength, acceleration, and pulling power for hills and mud.

Styling differs from make to make, but the basic layout remains much the same and the anatomy of the off-road racer shown here is typical of most bikes.

Throttle controls engine power

Fuel tank, designed not to leak if the bike crashes during a race. Fuel splashing over a hot engine is a fire hazard.

Rear mudguard

Exhaust pipe expels waste gases from the engine.

Foam-padded seat. Riders rarely sit when racing, as courses are usually far too bumpy!

Drive chain transfers power from the engine and gearbox to the rear wheel.

Shock absorber cushions the thud and bounce of off-road action.

Foot peg, one on each side

► Engine power is
controlled by a right-hand
twist-grip throttle.
Rolling the throttle back
gives more power. To
reduce it, the throttle is
eased forward.

Front mudguard

Front shock absorbers,
one in each of the two
front forks which join
the bike frame to the
front wheel.

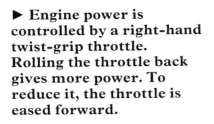

Engine, high-mounted
for good ground
clearance

Metal frame forms the
bike's backbone

Chunky-tread tire,
designed for maximum
grip on dirt surfaces

Inside the engine

■ Action begins in the engine when a mixture of fuel and air is sprayed into the top of the cylinder and ignited by a spark plug. This creates an explosion which forces the piston down the cylinder, as the diagrams on the right show. The piston's up-and-down movement is converted to a circular motion by a connecting rod and crankshaft and then to the rear wheel via a gearbox and chain (see page 38).

▶ Motorcycle engines come as two- or four-stroke designs. Two-strokes are often used in racing because they are light and powerful.

These diagrams show the basic principles of both engine types.

◀ This is a single-cylinder motorcycle engine. The black exhaust pipe sweeps up and is mounted high to avoid being damaged when the bike is tilted over in bends or bouncing through bumps.

Two stroke or four stroke?

Two-stroke engines get their name because the spark plug ignites the fuel every *second* vertical movement of the piston. This is called the power stroke.

Four-stroke engines work by a similar fuel explosion, but use one extra stroke to let the fuel in and another to expel waste gases. So the power stroke is every *fourth* piston movement.

Two-stroke engine

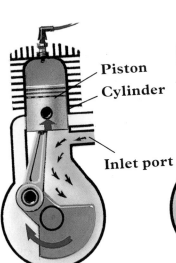

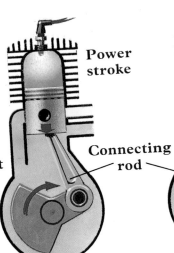

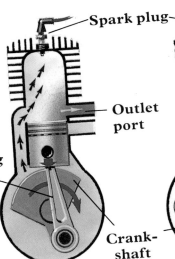

Spark plug

Piston
Cylinder

Power
stroke

Outlet
port

Inlet port

Connecting
rod

Crank-
shaft

Fuel is sucked in
as piston moves
up cylinder

Spark plug
ignites fuel,
forcing piston
down cylinder

As burned gases
go out of the
exhaust, fresh
fuel flows in
above piston

Piston moves
up ready for the
next power
stroke

Four-stroke engine

Inlet
valve

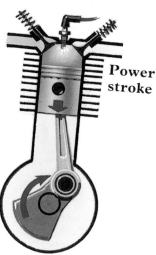

Exhaust
valve

Power
stroke

Fuel enters
cylinder via
intake valve

Piston moves
up cylinder

Spark plug
ignites fuel,
forcing piston
down cylinder

Piston moves up,
pushing burned
fuel out of
exhaust valve

Keeping on track

■ Off-road conditions demand tires with deep-cut chunky treads. On-road tires have fine-cut treads, designed for smooth, hard tarmac. They lose grip and spin uselessly if they sink into soft mud or sand.

Off-road wheels are usually spoked. The spokes cope with bumpy rough surfaces better than the solid cast alloy wheels of modern on-road motorcycles.

▶ Shock absorbers cushion the ride. Bikes either have a pair of shocks for each wheel, or a pair of shocks at the front with a single monoshock unit at the back.

The photograph far right shows a monoshock-equipped Suzuki moto-cross bike.

Front shock absorbers

Rear monoshock unit

On-road wheel and tire

The complex pattern cut into the rubber is designed to disperse rainwater, a slippery hazard on smooth tarmac. The tread goes round the sidewall, as on-road bikes lean over when cornering.

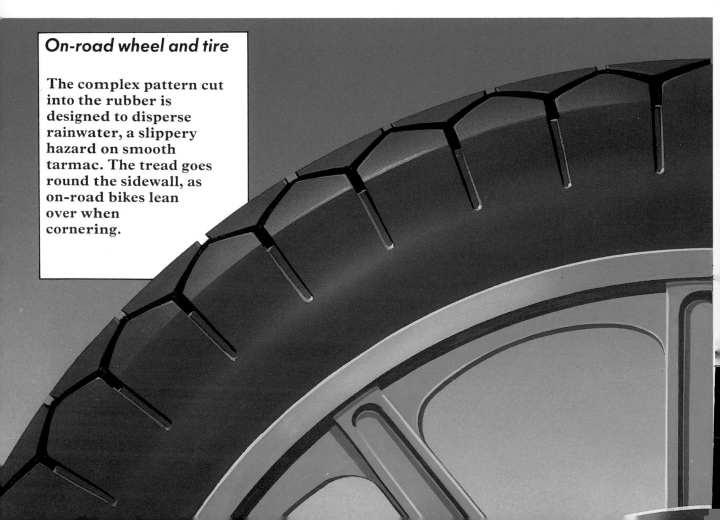

Off-road wheel and tire

Most off-roaders run on spoked wheels because the spokes have some give in them, so are better at absorbing bumps. The simple square pattern of the tire rubber gives excellent grip when riding on soft ground.

Safety helmets

■ The helmet is essential head protection and should always be worn on any motorcycle ride, no matter how short. Many off-road riders wear traditional, open-face helmets. For racing, a clip-on plastic face protector is worn to keep off muck and mud. Goggles with multi-layer transparent covers can be used. Each layer is ripped off as it gets dirty, so the rider has clear vision throughout a race.

► "Think safety" is common sense on a motorcycle. Even while practicing, this rider still wears his helmet and a full set of protective clothing.

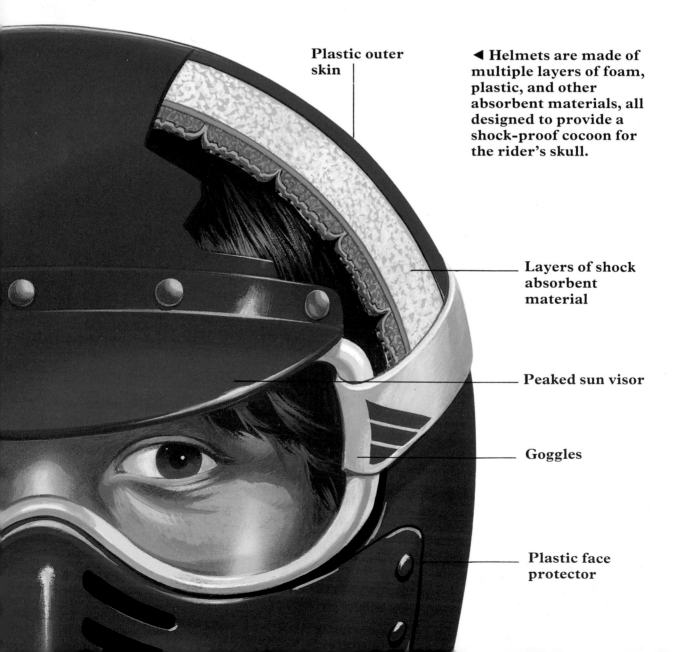

Plastic outer skin

◄ Helmets are made of multiple layers of foam, plastic, and other absorbent materials, all designed to provide a shock-proof cocoon for the rider's skull.

Layers of shock absorbent material

Peaked sun visor

Goggles

Plastic face protector

1920s pudding-basin helmet

Modern off-road helmet

Fully-enclosed helmet

◄ Helmets have come a long way since the early designs of the 1920s and 1930s. These first basin-shaped helmets were made of leather and cork.

In the 1950s, streamlined jet-style helmets were introduced, modeled on the aviation gear of the period.

The on-road bikers of today usually wear fully-enclosed helmets. Off-roaders mostly prefer the open-face jet style. All helmets have to comply with tough government safety standards.

Rider protection

■ Apart from a helmet, protective gear should always include tough gloves and boots — hands and feet are usually first to hit the ground when you fall off.

An important extra for motocross riders is body armor — plastic sections, shaped to cover and protect vulnerable areas such as the chest, shoulders and back, elbows, and knees.

▲ It's important to be dressed properly whenever you go out on a motorcycle, even if it's just for a spin down a country road. You never know when you might hit a patch of slippery mud and fall off — so whether riding fast or slow *always* wear protective gear, unlike this biker who demonstrates how *not* to do it!

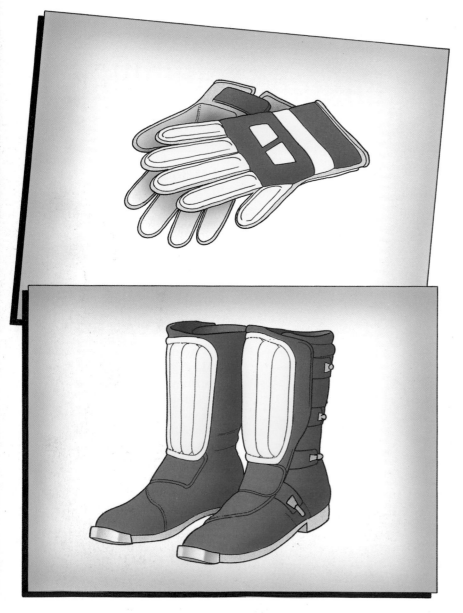

◀ Thick but supple leather is still the best all-round material for gloves and boots. Metal toecaps protect boot tips when scraping the ground.

Dressed for action!

This is how the well-dressed motorcycle rider looks, when wearing full protective gear for the motocross circuit. For ordinary trail biking, you don't need the racing colors or the super-tough body armor. Even so, you should always wear a proper helmet, tough jacket, full-length pants, and strong gloves and footwear.

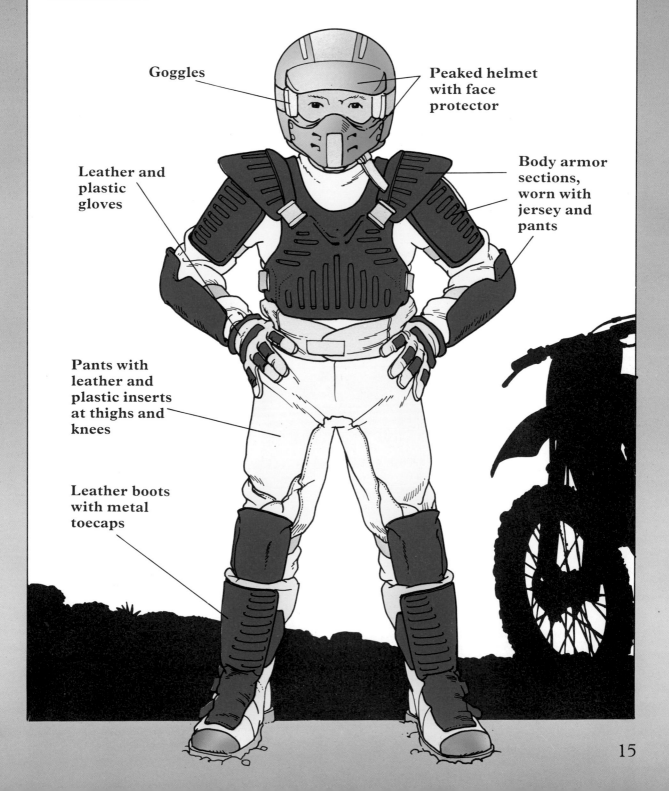

Goggles

Peaked helmet with face protector

Leather and plastic gloves

Body armor sections, worn with jersey and pants

Pants with leather and plastic inserts at thighs and knees

Leather boots with metal toecaps

At the controls

■ Riding a motorcycle is a job for both hands and both feet. The right hand controls the twist-grip throttle, with the fingers reaching forward to pull on the front-brake lever. The fingers of the left hand operate the clutch lever, pulling it in every time the gears are changed up or down.

On most bikes the left foot operates the gear-shift lever, and the right foot presses down to work the rear-brake lever.

► Gears are changed by tapping the gear lever up and down with your left foot with the clutch pulled in. A popular pattern for a five-gear bike is one down, four up — press the lever down for first gear, then hook your toe under and pull the lever up once for each further gear shift.

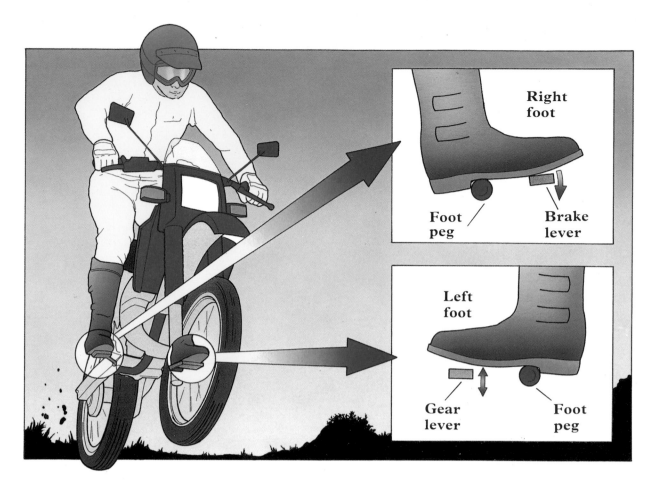

Right foot

Foot peg

Brake lever

Left foot

Gear lever

Foot peg

▲ The right foot presses down to work the rear brake lever. On motorcycles, front and rear brakes work independently. Normally they are used together to stop smoothly, but they can be used separately if required. But remember, a locked rear wheel can provoke a tailslide, and a locked front wheel can flip you off.

▼ Check the seat is at a comfortable height when choosing a bike. If you can't put your feet on the ground when sitting in the saddle, you can fall sideways if you halt on sloping ground.

◀ This motocross bike is stripped down to the bare minimum of controls. The clutch control lever is on the rider's left handlebar. On the other handlebar are the throttle and front brake. Down at foot level are the brake and gear levers.

To be driven on the highway, all bikes must have front and rear lights, direction indicators, speedometer, and horn.

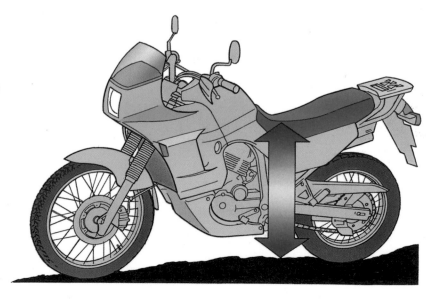

Taking care

■ Precision is the secret of successful trail bike riding, and speed is less important than being able to steer an exact path through deep ruts or over rocks and boulders. Practice by finding a smallish section of rough ground and riding a circuit on it — not in the fastest time, but seeing how slowly you can go. You'll be surprised how difficult slow riding can be!

Some trail machines

These machines are typical of the range of today's trail bikes. Most bikes are made by the Japanese big four: Honda, Suzuki, Yamaha, and Kawasaki. Other makers include Cagiva from Italy and BMW from West Germany.

Kawasaki KX125 G1 — good all-round bike, at home on roads or trails

Yamaha XT350 — light and easy to ride

Honda Transalp 600V — similar style to desert racers (page 32)

Cagiva Elefant 750 — Italian machine, good on the road, heavy off it

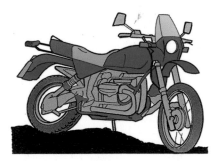

BMW R100GS — powerful West German twin-cylinder bike

Bike inspection

Motorcycles are unforgiving machines — if anything goes wrong, the rider usually gets hurt. That's why regular mechanical checks are essential.

   The most important safety checks are to the tires and brakes. Look over tires for nicks and cuts every time you go out, and check the air pressure in them daily or whenever you plan to go off-roading. Spokes tend to work loose or get bent in the rough, so inspect these regularly too.

   There's no need to go overboard with inspections. A thorough look takes only a few minutes, so it's easy to make a habit of checking the basics of your machine every time you plan to ride it.

Bike checklist

☑ Inspect tires for damage★
☑ Check tire pressures★★
☑ Are any wheel spokes bent or loose?★★
☑ Are horn, lights, and indicators adjusted and working?★
☑ How well are the brakes working?★
☑ Lubricate chain★★
☑ Check engine oil level★★
☑ Check fuel level★
☑ Are there any loose screws or bolts? Is anything missing?★

  ★ Whenever you ride
★★ Weekly or after a
    rough off-road ride

Personal checklist

☑ Helmet clean and undamaged★
☑ Helmet strap secure★
☑ Goggles or visor clean and unscratched★
☑ Boots, gloves, and clothes all in good condition★

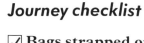

Journey checklist

☑ Bags strapped on securely★
☑ Bike loaded up as evenly as possible, so there isn't too much weight over front or back wheel★
☑ Tool kit aboard★
☑ Bottle of engine oil aboard (if you're going far)★
☑ Chain lubricant aboard★
☑ Tire repair kit aboard★

◄ Check the depth of large mud pools with a stick before you cross them . . .

Out in the wilds

■ Riding along remote tracks is a trail biker's dream, but even wild trails are likely to have some people on them, either walking or horse riding. Walkers don't like noisy motorcycles and horses are frightened by them, so keep the power low and slow down whenever you see people or animals.

It's illegal to ride motor vehicles on many rough trails, so rather than be stopped halfway by an angry landowner, check before you start.

▼ **Three trail bikers pause before crossing an old stone bridge.**

Rallies

These are a popular way to go long-distance riding in the company of other bikers. Many rallies just last a weekend and combine a fairly short ride with tenting and camp-fire cooking. Other rallies are in a different league altogether. The 1988 Paris–Nord Kapp rally, for instance, was a trip to the most northerly point in Europe. The route ran through eight countries and covered 4,000 miles. The scenery embraced empty beaches, remote valleys, and icy mountain ranges.

▲ Riders pause to rest on the beach at Lokken in Denmark. The van accompanied the bikes throughout, carrying spare baggage and equipment.

The trip to Norway's Nord Kapp (North Cape) was a one-make rally — all the bikers (179 people from 16 countries) rode twin-cylinder Honda Transalp trail bikes.

These machines proved very reliable, with few mechanical problems. However, there were lots of minor accidents — bumps, bruises, and some broken bones.

Motocross

■ The starter's flag drops and you're off. You hustle your bike round the course, flying through the air after bumps and pounding round bends, filling the air with the dust and dirt thrown up by your tires.

Motocross is the modern name for motorcycle scrambling, a sport that started in Britain. The first scramble was held in 1924.

▶ Motocross racers line up at the start, front tires against a metal gate. When this drops, the riders roar off, aiming to lead at the first bend, where the course narrows to a width of just a few feet.

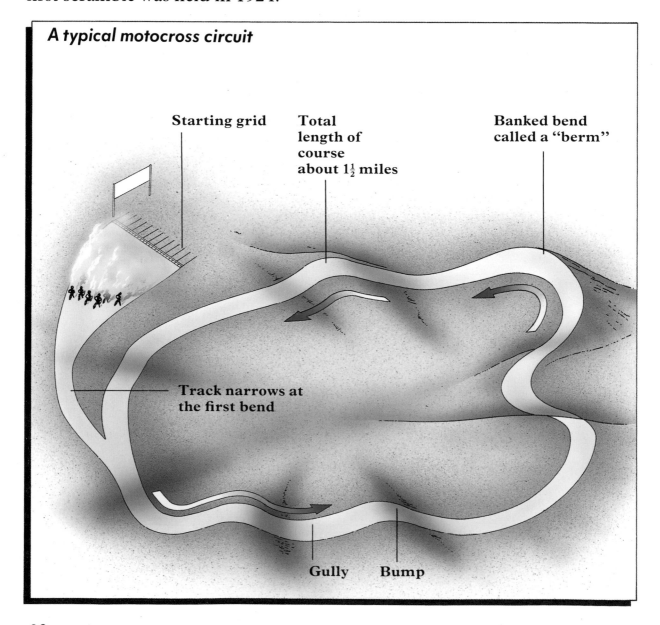

A typical motocross circuit

Starting grid

Total length of course about 1½ miles

Banked bend called a "berm"

Track narrows at the first bend

Gully   Bump

Riding to win

■ Motocross is an international sport with big prizes. The top teams are entered by bike manufacturers, with various sponsors putting up money in return for advertising space, both on the bikes and riders' clothing, and in the form of specially named race series.

There are various events for different engine sizes as well as races for young riders, who go on to adult events when they are old enough.

▼ Massed riders hurtle past the first bend. The leaders have a keen advantage here — the course is narrow and it can be difficult to overtake. Riders to the rear have to ride through a cloud of dirt and dust.

▼ The top riders are supported by teams of mechanics and helpers. Here a race instruction board is held up, giving details of a rider's position in the race.

► As in other forms of motor racing, a chequered flag is waved to signal the winner and the race end.

► Bike and rider fly through the air after a speed bump.

Motocross has given rise to many terms of speech which are unique to the sport, including "berm" for a banked-up bend and "holeshot" for the lead position gained by a rider within the first seconds of a race. Both of these terms have been borrowed by bicycle motocross and are used in BMX races everywhere.

On the beach

■ Beach racing can be as much a battle against gritty sand as against other riders. Sand clogs up everything, from chains and engines to boots, clothes, and helmets.

Dunes start out as steep climbs, but are gradually flattened as the bike tires plow them down into sand bogs.

Riders keep their weight to the rear of their machines — a front-heavy bike will dig into soft sand, throwing its rider onto the beach.

▶ In some races all types of off-road machine compete, including all-terrain vehicles (see page 35), motocross bikes, and bikes with sidecars.

In these races club riders have the chance to race against professional champions.

Sand racer's guide to the beach

Here are some practical hints and tips to improve your performance on the difficult terrain of a sandy beach:

MOTO-X IS GREAT!

Before the race, pull a pair of nylon tights over the engine air filter to keep out sand.

START

On straights, tuck your head down and elbows in. Keep your weight off the front.

On hard sand, sit toward the rear of the saddle.

Grab an early lead to make the most of the track — later riders have to cope with churned-up sand.

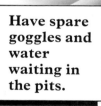

Have spare goggles and water waiting in the pits.

Use a smooth throttle action to avoid spinning the back wheel — it will dig down and the bike will get stuck.

On soft sand, stand on the foot pegs, but don't put too much weight on the handlebars and front wheel.

Don't ease off the power halfway up a dune — the bike will come to an instant halt and you'll have to get off and push it to the top.

In the early part of the race, taking steep dunes diagonally will make the slope gentler.

Supercross

■ Supercross is the stadium version of motocross. Riders compete in an indoor or outdoor stadium, with the dirt being brought in for the occasion and built into shape by bulldozers and earthmovers. The artificial track is often more difficult to negotiate than a natural course as the trucked-in material is quite soft. After the race, the earthmovers usually remove the track material.

▶ Three riders make spectacular jumps as they jostle for the lead. Supercross spectators have seats and don't have to stand in the muddy grass of a motocross circuit.

◀ An advantage of stadium riding is that night racing is possible, using powerful floodlights. Here a supercrosser rides a track in Los Angeles, California.

Trials events

■ These competitions are the opposite of fast-moving motocross racing, for trials test skill and balance. Speed is not essential but careful riding is. Routes for trials events include riverbeds, mountain sides and boulder-strewn gullies.

The aim is to complete each section of the course without stopping or putting a foot on the ground to keep your balance.

▼ Trials courses are divided into obstacle sections of various lengths. Some really difficult sections last only 70 to 100 feet, but others may be ten times as long.

▲ Riders lose points if they put a foot on the ground to keep balance. Called "dabbing," this earns one penalty point. A rider whose engine stops gets five penalty points.

▶ Trials bikes are equipped with super-low "crawler" gears, to enable them to move very slowly without the engine snatching or stalling.

Enduro!

■ Enduros are the toughest long-distance races in the world. Riders combat time and rough country as they battle to complete each stage. Penalty points are awarded for lateness, and even if the riders are early!

Long enduros include the Baja 1000, which runs through the searing heat of the Baja peninsula in Mexico. Riders in Australia's Wynns Safari battle through desert, rainforests, and crocodile-infested swamps. The Paris-Dakar rally includes navigation stages through desert regions, and there are always some competitors who get lost . . .

▶ One important rule for Paris–Dakar riders is to keep the advertising badges stuck on their machines clean at all times. This is so they will show up on news photographs and video reporting for television!

▼ This Paris–Dakar rider was overcome by desert heat for a while before carrying on in the race. Machines need to be reliable, as during each stage competitors have to carry out running repairs themselves, using whatever on-board equipment they can carry.

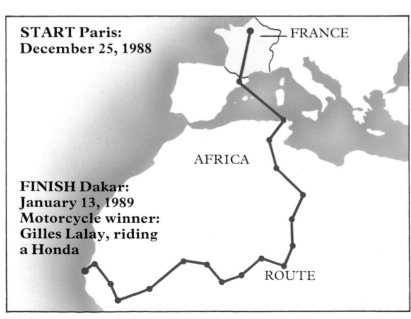

START Paris:
December 25, 1988

FINISH Dakar:
January 13, 1989
Motorcycle winner:
Gilles Lalay, riding
a Honda

FRANCE

AFRICA

ROUTE

◄ After its start in France, the Paris–Dakar rally runs through much of northwest Africa and the Sahara desert. This map shows the 1988/89 route — each year the course is slightly different.

The Paris–Dakar lasts nearly three weeks and can be dangerous in parts. There are always some casualties.

Other off-road races

■ Other off-road events include grass track racing. Here, riders use lightweight bikes, racing around roughly oval circuits. Riders use their feet to balance their bikes as they speed along on the slippery surface.

As in motocross, riders can start young in grass track racing. Boys and girls of six years and up can join clubs to get expert tuition and take part in fierce competitions.

▼ **Grass track racers roar round circuits in groups of eight riders at a time. In fact, "grass track" is rather overstated — after the first few laps the grass is worn away and the race becomes a dirt scramble.**

All-terrain vehicles

Called ATVs for short, these are equipped with wide, "doughnut" tires. They were originally designed as go-anywhere buggies for farmers, but it wasn't long before ATVs were being raced.

ATVs come in three- and four-wheel versions, and they demand a special riding style. Riders have to lean hard over in corners to balance the machines. In mud, without lots of weight to one side, an ATV will slide straight on instead of turning the way you planned!

ATVs are great fun to ride, but three-wheelers are now banned in some countries because there have been so many accidents involving them.

Three-wheel ATV

Four-wheel ATV

Squashy doughnut tires

▼ A rider powers his way through a turn on a four-wheel ATV.

Action photography

The secret of taking good pictures at a motocross race lies in getting as close as possible to the action. Luckily, at most meetings you can do just that, since the barrier tapes are rarely more than a few yards from the track.

If your camera has variable shutter speeds use a fast one — 1/250 second exposure should give crisp shots of fast-moving bikes, if you pan the camera to follow your subject.

▼ An SLR (single-lens reflex) camera is ideal for sports photography, as you can change the lens to suit the subject. Many of the newer SLR cameras have special settings, designed to focus on fast-moving objects.

◄ Compact cameras are pocket sized and suitable for many general shots. Some expensive compacts have a built-in telephoto lens, which can be used to take close-ups of individuals.

Close to the action

Telephoto lenses enable you to get close-up shots, but because it is difficult to hold long lenses steady you run the risk of blurred pictures.

A 400 mm telephoto lens is about the longest you can use for hand-held shots. To keep things as steady as possible, hug your arms against your chest and hold your breath as you press the camera shutter.

For rock-steady support, use a tripod

Hold the camera firmly when using a telephoto lens

► Try and fill the frame with the subject — few shots are more boring than those showing tiny riders, lost in a big landscape.

◄ Note how the high shutter speed used for this photo shows clods of earth, apparently frozen in mid-air. Even so, the rear wheel has a slight blur, giving an impression of speed.

Tech talk

■ Here is a glossary of the technical words found in this book, together with some biker expressions.

ATV
All-terrain vehicle — an off-road buggy which runs on squashy, "doughnut" tires.

Berm
Banked-up bend on a motocross course.

BMX
Bicycle motocross — cyclists race round a rough track, on small-wheeled bicycles instead of on motorbikes.

Chequered flag
Black-and-white flag used to signal the winner and the end of the race.

Clutch
Operated by pulling the left handlebar lever, the clutch disengages the engine from the gearbox when changing gears.

Crankshaft
Metal shaft at the bottom of the engine, which is joined to the connecting rod. The "con rod" transfers the up-and-down movement of the piston to the rotating crankshaft.

Drive chain
Metal chain connecting gearbox to rear wheel.

Enduro
Long-distance race through rough country. Trail bikes styled after enduro machines have become popular in recent years. Typically, these have a powerful engine, long-range fuel tank and a mini-windscreen and streamlined headlight.

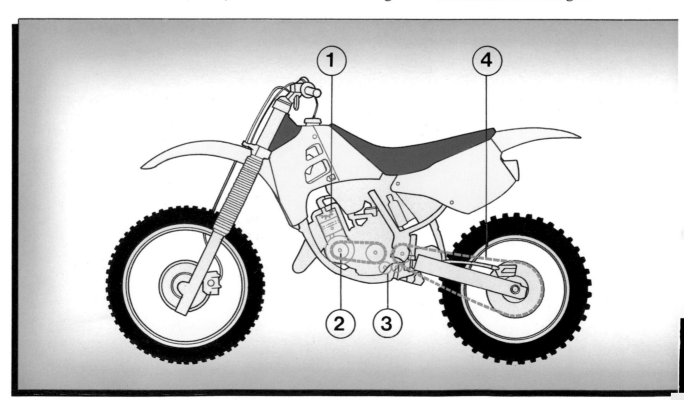

Gearbox

This transfers power from the crankshaft to the drive chain. Use low gear for starting, then switch to higher gears as the bike accelerates, changing down for hills and when slowing down or stopping.

Holeshot

A motocross rider who grabs the lead for the first bend has the holeshot.

Motocross

A race over bumpy ground. In events made up of a number of heats, each race is called a moto.

Shock absorber

Often nicknamed "shocker." Metal springs in an oil- or air-filled tube which cushion a bike's movement.

Blaze of power

This is how power is transferred from engine to rear wheel.

1. Inside the engine, the piston moves up and down the cylinder.
2. The piston is attached to the connecting rod which turns the crankshaft.
3. The crankshaft is connected by a chain to the gearbox. High (fast) or low (slow) gears are selected by the rider.
4. The drive chain turns the rear wheel. Some bikes have a shaft in place of a drive chain.

Spark plug

This provides the electric spark that ignites the fuel-air mixture in the cylinder. The resulting explosion forces the piston down the cylinder.

Speedometer

Instrument to show ground speed.

Sponsor

A person or company who backs a race or racing team with money in exchange for publicity.

Supercross

Motocross races held in an indoor or outdoor stadium. A course is specially built for each event, then cleared away afterward.

Tachometer

Instrument to show engine revolutions per minute.

Throttle

Twist-grip control which varies engine speed.

▲ The monoshocks on these motocross bikes are much lighter than the traditional pair of rear shock absorbers.

Trail bike

Motorcycle built to travel on- or off-road. To be street-legal, it must have horn, lights, indicators, and speedometer.

Tread

Pattern cut or molded into a tire to improve grip. On-road tires have complex tread patterns.

Off-road tires have simple square-cut treads to grip on soft surfaces such as sand or mud.

Trials

A stadium event involving a course made up of natural obstacles.

Arena trials are held indoors or outdoors. Typical obstacles include oil cans, slippery planks, and old cars.

Index